We Like to Eat Well

We Like to Eat Well

ELYSE APRIL

Illustrated by Lewis Agrell

Family Health Series

KALINDI PRESS
Prescott, Arizona

Cover design: The Agrell Group: www.theagrellgroup.com
Book design: The Agrell Group, lagrell@commspeed.net
Book layout: Kadak Graphics, www.kadakgraphics.com

ISBN: 978-1-935826-04-0

KALINDI PRESS
P.O. Box 1589
Prescott, AZ 86302
800-381-2700
www.kalindipress.com

This book was printed in China.

For Paul

We like to eat fresh.

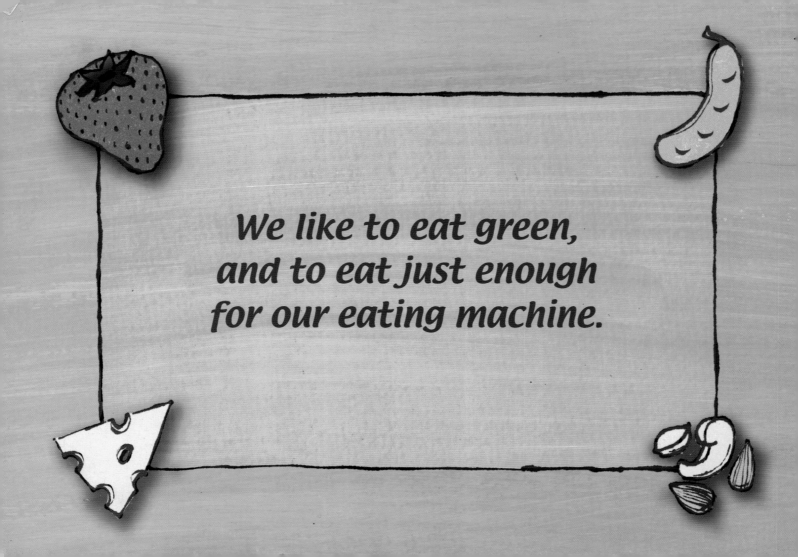

We like to eat green,
and to eat just enough
for our eating machine.

We like to eat chewy,
we like to eat smooth.

We like to eat sitting
or while on the move.

We like eating together;
we like eating slow.

We like to try new things
and foods that we know.

We like to eat colors ...

... and all kinds of shapes.
We like eating whole foods
or slices and flakes.

We like to eat sweet ...

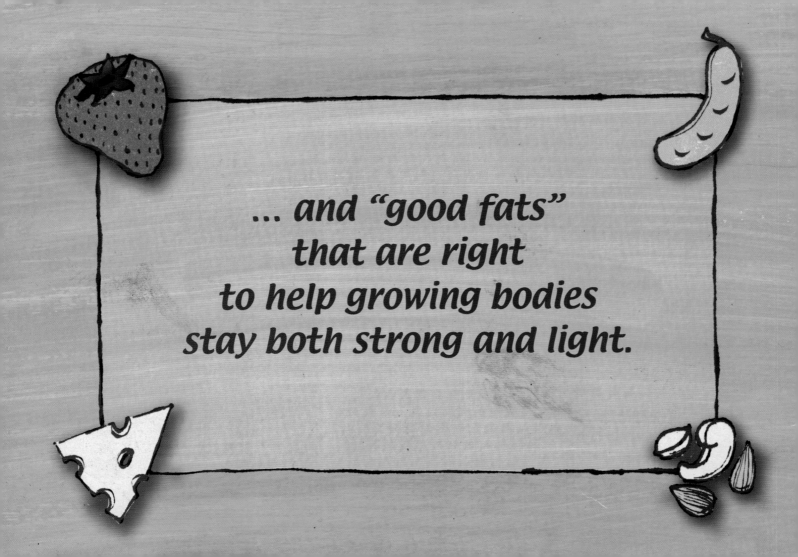

... and "good fats"
that are right
to help growing bodies
stay both strong and light.

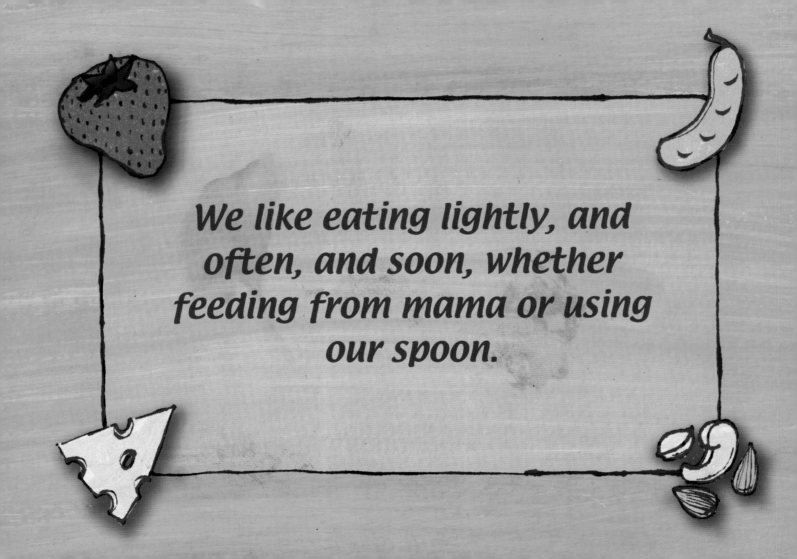

We like eating lightly, and often, and soon, whether feeding from mama or using our spoon.

We like to eat warm and we like to eat cool. We can eat well at home, we can eat well at school.

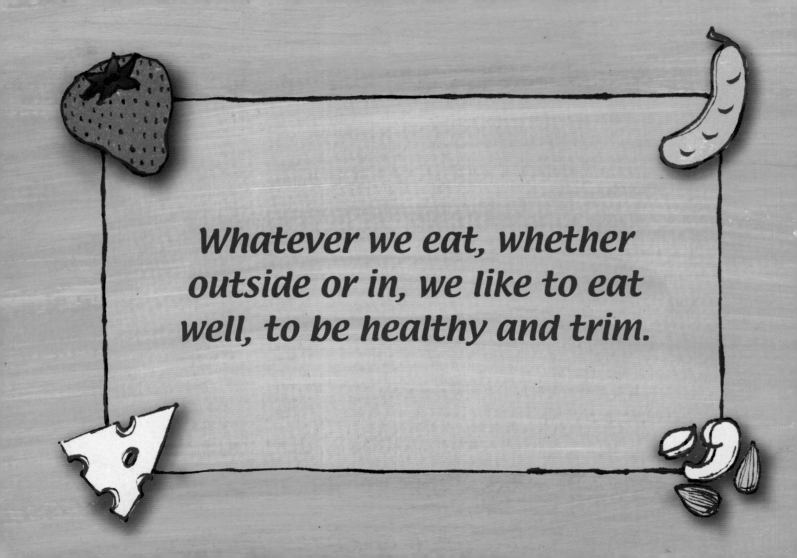

Whatever we eat, whether outside or in, we like to eat well, to be healthy and trim.

OTHER FAMILY HEALTH TITLES FROM KALINDI PRESS

We Like To Play Music
by Kate Parker
Design by Zachary Parker
This easy-to-read picture book is full of photos of children playing music, moving to a beat and enjoying music alone or with parents or peers.
ISBN: 978-1-890772-85-7, paper, 32 pages, $9.95
Spanish Language Version: *Nos Gusta Tocar Música*
ISBN: 978-1-890772-90-1

We Like To Help Cook
by Marcus Allsop
Illustrations by Diane Iverson
Based on the USDA Food Pyramid guidelines, young children help adults to prepare healthy, delicious foods. (Ages: 2-6)
ISBN: 978-890772-70-3, paper, 32 pages, $9.95
Spanish Language Version: *Nos Gusta Ayudar a Cocinar*
ISBN: 978-1-890772-75-8

We Like To Move: Exercise Is Fun
by Elyse April
Illustrations by Diane Iverson
This vividly-colored picture book encourages exercise as a prescription against obesity and diabetes in young children. (Ages: Infants-6)
ISBN: 978-890772-60-4, paper, 32 pages, $9.95
Spanish Language Version: *Nos Gusta Movernos: El Ejercicio Es Divertido* ISBN: 978-890772-65-9

We Like To Live Green
by Mary Young
Design by Zachary Parker
This Earth-friendly book provides an introduction to vital environmental themes in ways that will appeal to both young children and adults.
ISBN: 978-1-935387-00-8, paper, 32 pages, $9.95
Spanish Language Version: *Nos Gusta Vivir Verde*
ISBN: 978-1-935387-01-5

TO ORDER: 800-381-2700, or visit our website, www.kalindipress.com *Special discounts for bulk orders.*